EVERGREEN

POEMS

CHRISTIE LEIGH BABIRAD

ISBN: 979-8-3303-3241-0

Published in the United States of America by Harbor Lane Books, LLC.

www.harborlanebooks.com

Evergreen is dedicated to the "Evergreen" individuals in my life, old and new, who are unwavering in their love and are the guiding light behind everything I create and put forth with my entire heart.

PREFACE

Evergreen: (adjective) from Merriam-Webster
• Having foliage that remains green and functional through more than one growing season.
• Universally and continually relevant

Evergreen is a metaphor for this collection. I wanted these poems to embody the quest in life to find that which is evergreen, whether it be through our imaginations and what stirs us to believe in something more, or through the serendipitous finding of love that stands the test of time.

CONDUIT OF LOVE

To light the dark night.
To ignite a hopeless heart.
When love has gone away,
I would like to change the view,
To be that smile one needs.

WHEN YOU KNOW HOW LUCKY
YOU ARE

When you know how lucky you are,
You're holding onto every moment like it's the last.
Like Hearing
Your mom playing on the black and white keys in the
living room
The same songs that were played when you were a little girl.
Like Feeling
The one you truly believe could be "the one"
Pulling you in close with no desire to let go.
Like Seeing
All the city and Christmas lights sparkling before you,
Reminding you of how alive with potential you truly are.
Like Tasting
Hot chocolate on the coldest winter night,
Sweetness and heat filling your soul with such comfort
and joy.
And when you know how lucky you are,
You've also most likely felt, tasted, heard, and seen how love
leaves.
But, if you have known how lucky you are,

You've held onto every moment like it was the last,
Making this love
A part of you,
Never completely gone,
Lingering viscerally and profoundly,
Beyond any difficult times.
And you know
In the deepest crevice of your heart
How very lucky you are
To be living this life.

SPRINGTIME'S SONG

A song of uncovering,
Opening up
To saturated pink and yellow,
From tulips to Easter egg coloring.
Little green shoots rise from dark soil.
Ideas stir with the birds in the trees,
With that first bite into the sweetest clementine.
Spring is a melody of instinctual knowing
There is a remarkable journey before you.
It is a season and a song not unlike fall,
Heralding desire,
Sparking the urge to start new,
To move toward the sun
And never sought before wishes and dreams.

MY GUARDIAN WOLF PACK

The wolves came when my eyelids closed last night.
My mind had been filled with flurries of fearful what-if's,
But then these wolves gathered around me.
They were gentle and wanted to stay.
They followed me to my door,
Encouraged me to play,
And would not leave my side.
When I later looked up this dream of mine,
I found that wolves represent protection and family.
I believe this to be a sign, a reminder;
There will always be angels that belong to you,
Surrounding you when you need them.
Mine came in the form of a pack of wolves,
My angels that I will keep in my heart's memory,
To recall whenever I feel those unnecessary fears coming
back to me.

A VISIT TO THE WISHING WELL

I wore my favorite long burgundy velvet dress and went to the wishing well today, deep in a forest of towering oaks and pines, and thick leafy plants that extended onto the tightrope-thin path. Made from solid wood that turned to silver over time, I kneeled beside this pail and put forth my wish in a prayer, to be happy in the present. I wished to remember that many have walked this life before I, and many will do so after. And, many before have gone through what seemed insurmountable and triumphed, as will I. I then took in the stillness that could not have been afforded had I made my wish at the flowing fountain nearby, and I said thank you to the well and forest that moments like this can still be found in a world as chaotic and disorienting as the one we currently live within.

LA LUNA

La Luna tonight,
glows softly,
showing me the way.

RECAPTURED

She is a girl running into the ocean before the next wave,
Waiting for the right moment to freestyle her strong little arms,
And sail,
Back to the shore.
Sand and possibly a string of broccoli-colored seaweed in her hair,
Water dripping down her iridescent soft-pink bathing suit,
Energy coursing through her limbs;
She wipes the salt water from her bright brown eyes,
Ready to race back into the fun,
Wholeheartedly unconcerned by the trappings of appearance—
A moving picture of what happiness and freedom look like.

MORNING VISION

I woke up today with a beautiful vision.
There was a scattering of glitter around a pearl-painted
castle in the distance.
The sky was a vibrant mid-afternoon blue.
And the trees, surrounding but not crowding, were emerald.
And I thought to myself,
Since I have not woken to this vision before—
Maybe not since I was a little girl;
I could think of this vision as a sign,
A metaphor for my dreams,
That maybe all that I am currently wishing for is not as far
away as it seems.

GRAND FATHER

She remembers him,
The one who was always present,
Standing beside the middle school track on rain-soaked spring afternoons
To clap for his granddaughter racing for her personal best.
He never attended out of obligation.
That's not what she felt.
He was there for her to truly see that she was special to him,
That he believed in her like no one else.
She still remembers him,
His memory not fading in the least.
He was the one who was always present,
Standing beside her on cold Christmas Eve nights,
White-stemmed candles in gloved hands,
Singing "Silent Night" in front of the church's manger.
He was always there to imprint the importance of tradition and moments on her heart.
And she now sees that this was all so she would never feel alone.
She remembers him,

And she could never forget him,
For he was a "Grand Father,"
The man who was always present.
And from Heaven, he remains her guide to this day.
He is the one who is and has always been beside her.

A PRAYER

May this day stretch—
Far beyond the capsuled hours,
With summertime sunshine,
And the fragrance of acres upon acres of newly bloomed red
roses
On a nearby sea breeze.

VISUAL AFFIRMATION

Blush pink rose,
Petals outstretched,
Like a ballerina
Standing out in a row,
Different from all the rest,
An affirmation of peace in an uneven place.

TRUSTED THE MOMENT

When we were children
We trusted the moment,
Sleeping over in new friends' places,
Allowing legends and stories to take us in and away,
Wherever they may.

THE SPARKLING ONE

My out-of-this-world love for my mom has been difficult to
put into lines,
though I have tried countless times.
I think of the late nineties Rainforest Café right now,
Leaving one place for another through creativity and imag-
ination,
A representation of what she has established for me.
She gave me an internal ability to always have a place for my
heart to go,
An ingrained knowledge from her that there is always hope.
In reflecting on your sweetest memories,
This is what can transport you into the next steps of your
reality;
She taught me.
And I think of all the other school field trips with my mom,
How I wanted to be with her, rather than my peers,
Not because she was my mom,
Simply because she had more wonder and fun.
My mom brings every moment to greater life.

She is "The Sparkling One" in everything she is and does.
And she has taught me how to remain bright,
In a world that often tries to dim your light.

CHOSEN MEDIUM

This must be right,
For when I am in the deepest depths of despair,
Putting my feelings onto the page gives me that breath of
fresh air.
A light within clicks on, sparking lines only my heart could
tell,
And down I fall into what feels like a specially made-for-me,
glittering, magic well.

LIFE THROUGH A CHILD'S HEART

Today I saw a snowman made from the tiniest storm,
top hat and bright red scarf,
standing on slightly coated grass.
And as I drove by, I thought—
This creation out of seemingly little,
This is the greatest depiction of how we should live each day,
With the seeing eyes of a child creating a snowman from the
smallest amount of snow.
I strive to view my life forward this way,
Because when the rain falls, children splash around in
puddles,
Reveling in the splat sound and the sight of the water flying
upward the harder they stomp.
In the sunshine, they race back and forth across dew-wet
fields,
Tossing off their coats with such wild abandon and pure joy.
And on cloudy days, they're coming up with ghost stories
and intricate forts.
Children live each moment.
Life is not short from a child's view.

And it is time that I live my life
Again, through the brilliant and visionary eyes and heart of a
child;
It is the only way to ensure a life that is truly and completely
lived.

THE RUNNER

With the rising sun,
Red trails through every vein of my body,
Awakening me.
Legs push in first strides,
Until falling into a pace.
Early morning air enters my lungs.
A playlist of current thoughts smoothly jog through my
mind,
In and out,
Sometimes staying on specific tracks,
Until clarity is achieved.
Answers are always given with this movement and time,
As a gentle breeze travels through my hair,
My pony-tail swinging back and forth,
And warm rays stream across my face.
My breathing is steady yet challenged.
And I always feel stronger upon completion,
In body and mind.
With this running routine of mine,
I am filled up with gratitude each time.

WHAT MAKES US

Feelings
Sparkle, Destroy
Running, Swaying, Weaving
Like a wave, you can't stop the rise
Caring, Believing
Living

THE HEART SPEAKS

The heart speaks.
To roads you are meant to take.
Adventures you are meant to experience.
To love that is intended to help you bloom.
The heart does not promise forever,
but will never lead you astray.
The heart is an unwavering advocate,
here to remind you that you are alive.
The heart speaks,
and we could all use a good consistent listen to what she has
to say,
each day and night.

LIGHT BLUE

His love is light blue
The color of the sky absent a single cloud
The color of the sea sans a single wave
This is not to describe perfection
For that will never be what she seeks
But it is a love that shows and does
Through his strength of spirit
His faith that is unspoken but apparent in the way he moves
His calm
His steady presence
His consistent care
Her never failing to mention his charm
He has a way of bringing incomparable joy to her heart
It is a love that has her feeling both connected and free
Beyond open to life and all its possibilities
More prepared for life's challenges
His love has her dreaming more
Certain in his love
At greater peace in this ocean of life

Heart-filled now with what she wanted all along
Unwaveringly present in this truth
Deep healing breaths
In this light blue love of hers

WISHING FOR STEADY GROUND

Where is your heart?
Here is to praying that it is on the same line as mine.

A WISH FOR A SLOW DOWN

I want to slow down with you,
Take the long way home,
Moving in our own way,
In our own time,
A pace we create,
Just you and me.

This life has been spinning way too fast.
I ache too often with the missing you.
Late-night mind wanderings
Take me to hopeful bliss,
Or consumed by what-if's ruin.

Round and round,
I need for the clock to stop,
If only in my heart.
To feel the spring sunshine on my neck through rolled-down
windows,
With your hand wrapped around mine,
And nowhere to be for a long while.

WAVES OF EMOTION

Waves of emotion
Roll,
Glide,
Crash
Over me.
Their force at times disorienting,
Swallowing my mortal coil whole.
Yet, always temporary these waves are,
Passing with the breeze.
I must remember,
When fears and self-imposed inadequacy overtake me.
I remind myself,
This is life,
In all its confusion, chaos,
Wonder.

NEW IDENTITY

She stepped off her horse so high,
a place of safety from the fears she tries to hide.
Swiftly running out of the fiery forest that used to inflame
her desire to do more, be more;
she stops at the oceanside
where the fish swim free in a dance.
And her heart calms
with a knowing
she has found her next home
to grow,
to begin again
with her feet firmly in the sand and ankle-deep water.

IT'S A CHOICE

Do I get lonely?
Of course.
All of the time.
But my peace is worth more,
More than the risk of provoking and stirring the spirits of
lost earthly beings.

LIFE'S TUG

Her life has been feeling like a racetrack.
Moments she tries to capture are blurred,
Like a snapshot of fall leaves on trees when the car is moving
too fast.
Mornings swiftly sweep away to night,
With not enough, if any, life-path markers to show she is
truly living each day.
Months and years turn as quickly as they begin,
And her anxiety often sees the scarecrow on her road,
His stance still,
And these days he is no longer pointing in every direction.

EVERGREEN

I need something I can hold onto,
Someone who does not change with the wind's temper,
Someone Evergreen
Like the tall tree,
A soul who breathes into me a balance of life
To no longer be continually purpose-driving in this life
alone.

ARCHIVIST

She's an archivist with her moments.
The scenes that could never be captured by film,
She stows through her poetry.
Like when he looked over at her after a noticeably beaming
older couple greeted and passed them on the autumn-leafed
trail—
The way his eyes sparkled among the open field of crimson
wildflowers,
And the boyish smile he had that was undeniably genuine—
That held meaning,
That held an unspoken truth—
Maybe even a promise.

A NEW PICTURE

I had someone in my life who would speak of "the bubble" as this place you would enclose yourself in when you were in love or sparked by the muse. "The bubble" was a protective space. Yet now, I think of "the bubble" as more of a home—a locale of freedom that is always within us. It is a place we can and should repeatedly return to. "The bubble" is a place of belief, overjoyed emotions, and ignited passions we should never stray far from— a place of reminder to not lose the light and connection we have built into our individual lives.

A DIFFERENT KIND OF CLOSURE

He returns through her dreams,
A repeated figure in a different storyline each time.
But always a constant,
He is back in the image she wished he could have stayed in.
And he is sorry.
Scenes shaded in a late autumn sky,
Melancholy mixed with the greatest belief
Stretching through the black night and into the daylight.

KEEP MOVING

There is a drumbeat inside her,
At the center of her chest.
It is a sound of instinctual knowing.
The beat is louder in volume at times,
Traveling through a late autumn whistle in the wind,
Among tall trees losing their leaves,
And red and orange shapes dancing down from the blue sky
above at a perfectly measured pace.
This drumbeat playing within her is a reminder,
A calling—
With certainty to remember,
This life in all actuality is factually magical.
And there's almost a desperate demand in the chilled air,
For her to keep her eyes and heart wide open,
Past the non-believers and non-seekers who all too often
surround.

TRUST

Much of what she feared
Covered the forest of her soul in fog,
Leading her to simply keep moving forward;
No answers,
Only trust
As her fears turned the fog to night,
And the worry that weighed heaviest
To the yellow fireflies' glow.
Seemingly a reassurance,
What she feared the most at this time holds great light,
"Should the fates allow."
And she is guided
To continue moving forward,
Believing,
Her story will be better than anything she could have ever
planned or controlled.

LIFE IS FRAGILE

Life is fragile.
I prefer this to "short."
It is more precise.
Life is fragile,
Like the spark of an idea
If not written down
Is often gone;
And our moments,
If not cherished and implanted in our memory
like seeds,
Will most often disappear
along with our greatest path forward.

THE WAY SHE MOVES

She speaks in lyrics.
Natural.
Never rehearsed.
She feels life through story and a soft melody.
She breaks with the sound of glass.
She falls in love with the sky shading into sunset colors.
Love songs always hit her differently,
Stopping her in her tracks,
The heart of it all completely silencing the world around her.

NOSTALGIC AND GENUINELY TRUE

She dreams
In iridescent pink satin
And velvets of ruby and royal blue,
A remembrance of her childhood;
The puzzle piece to what she longs for
And what remains true
To her soul and entire being to this day.

TIME'S KEEPER

Time has not changed.
It does not speed up or slow down.
Time only serves as a reminder
to breathe deep,
focused and slow,
in and out,
to listen,
release the hurt that creates the illusion you are a prisoner to
this intangible subject.
And take in all that you value,
the moments that have enriched your heart.
Time encourages action;
Speaking through a breeze on the wind,
through the sunlight that shines on the water like crystals—
"You are the magical fairy to your soul."
"You are your Time's Keeper."

FLOWER CHILDREN

Maybe we are all "Flower Children"
If only we truly took in one magical season we were given
And learned to keep that desire for freedom and light
within us.

THE PROMISE

Rooted
In the earth's soil,
Spring's sun on winter-adjusted skin,
The visceral remembrance of nature's endless blessings,
Life's eternal hope.

WILDFLOWERS

Take me back
To a lullaby melody.
We don't need to always be saying so much.
Sometimes it's sweet to hear what has been true all along.
True love requires no reason—
A picture of bright little flowers some may call weeds
In a field that goes beyond what the eyes can see
Under a bright-summer-blue sky,
The deepest souls touched,
The sun shining on tall stalks of golden reeds.

GROWING UP

Growing up—
It's taking hold of your integrity and personal responsi-
bilities,
Keeping alive your child-seeded identity,
While society often inundates you with numerous contra-
dictions.
I believe this is growing up—
As in, "Growing upward"
In your purpose,
In the cultivation of a most fulfilled and joyful life.

FULFILLED

You have her smiling in the middle of the day,
Feeling warm sunlight traveling through her entire body,
Her mind filled with hope and belief,
With real-life visions
Of sparkles,
Soft velvet,
And wonder that lasts beyond holiday seasons.

WHAT HE SAYS ABOUT YOU

I picture you beside a white-lit Christmas tree
even though we have never met.
I picture you looking down at the earth that holds your
husband.
And you can hear what he says about you,
a smile on your face that stretches to your glistening-with-
joy eyes.
He says you gave with your whole heart.
You thought of everyone else above yourself.
Helping others brought you the greatest joy.
A crack in his voice,
I could hear both emptiness and fullness in him across the
line.
When he spoke of you he showed me a selfless life,
one filled with genuine love that is everlasting.
The love that you shared,
the greatest gift of all.
I hope you can feel him
forever tied to you,

forever in love with you
'til the fates bring you back together again.

INDIGO

Not of the daily grind,
Where a girl's dreams live,
In a time of starlight.

STORYTIME

Fill her with stories as deep as the tangled tree-canopied
forest.
Accompanied by the orchestra of Stephen Sondheim;
Captured is mystery, isolation, hope, strength, and of
course—
love.
To once again recall
The heroine within,
A girl who always stood tall, assured, and brave,
Armed the archer when need be.
She will now be ready to step forward,
Only having needed a reminder of who she was born to be.

TIME OUT

She needs a little more magic in her days—
A red dress slow dance with her love
In that cozy Speakeasy-style bar in the middle of the city,
Only the piano and saxophone playing on the stage.
Or maybe a weekend of being snowed-in,
Only the Christmas and snow-light,
A fresh pot of hazelnut coffee steaming in the kitchen
To be fireside wrapped in a blanket to be shared,
Reading poetry while glancing out the nearby frosted
windowpanes.

WHAT IS TRUE

The sun rising each morning whether bright or hidden by
clouds.
A baby wrapping its fingers around yours.
An older dog with faded fur wagging its tail for you.
The way the trees' branches sway with the wind.
The love you say "yes" to and feel both excitement and
contentment when making plans.
The distinct feel of a loved one's embrace.
The spark within you that guides you into something
sparkling and fantastically new.

TOGETHER, ALONE

One heart.
One soul.
One body.
Complete in the desire and giving of love.
Committing this holiday season to herself.
How she moves.
How she indulges.
And how she reaches out to more than one person.
Feeling whole and together.
Alone with herself.
One woman.
Recognizing the radiant light she possesses.
Fully capable of spreading this light in her own unique way.
Irreplaceable.
Holding the faith to reach further and wider than she could
have imagined before.

VALIDATION

She was the girl who wanted to show everyone how she
twirled in her brand-new dress,
How she decorated her room,
What she loved.
Now looking back on the girl she was, she realizes she hasn't
traveled far.
She still wants to feel accepted and loved by everyone else.
That's what it was.
And she still to this day desires that validation,
That she is more than enough,
That she is essential,
Maybe even that bright light in the darkness for someone
else,
That one someone who makes them feel more than vali-
dated, too.

IN THE WOODS

Disoriented;
Moving on vision alone,
To her bold purpose.

TURNING OVER A NEW LEAF

Turning over leaves,
Only one has her answer
On a new journey.

LOTTERY WINNER

If I won all the gold,
To this daily life I would fold.
And to the forest I would be sold,
Where the creative life is encouraged and not seen as a path
that is bold.

WAR

Reporters rattle off numbers and removed-from-the-heart details
As the people at a perceived safe distance become desensitized,
Sharing the news in the same breath as what's happening on their favorite television show,
While those of us aware are continually pushing beyond the anxiety we feel for the widely immoral and removed-from-God society in which we live.

CONTEMPLATION

Autumn trees shimmer in the sunlight.
Driving down this highway,
There are few cars on the road this early.
And my thoughts wander.
Am I on track?
Or have I suddenly realized,
I have been moving through the woods of my life with trust?
Maybe I am lost.
But maybe I am okay;
Taking this story of mine one place at a time,
Driving completely open to the seasons and unknown
changes ahead
With faith, heart, and strength ingrained in my soul.

Pen poised at the blank page;
She wonders if others are feeling the same as she,
That this world is seemingly more rushed,
And its people more spiritually detached than ever before.
And if so, maybe this is something for her to say.
If many feel the same way,
Maybe through her expression,
Connections can be made.
And as a collective of seekers,
Slower movement will be the way.
The ones who recognize the matrix they have caught them-
selves in will set themselves free,
And they will be able to open their hearts to the goodness
that can now come their way.

THANKSGIVING

You and me.
A walk parallel to the late fall shoreline.
Casper blue sky.
A crisp wind moving through us.
Instinct speaking soft but assured of a future we will share.

YOU ARE MY EVERGREEN

I know I love you is an overused phrase.
Maybe you do not think I could truly feel that way about
you yet,
That it is just something a girl can so easily say.
But you would be wrong.
I have thought about this more than you realize.
I love you.
And this is not hinged on you returning this phrase to me.
I love you for the way you care with your entire heart.
How you wanted to look into my eyes that day and make
sure I was okay.
The way you call and text after every date.
The way you jump from topic to topic when something
suddenly comes to your mind.
The way you laugh.
The way you flirt.
The way you return to the car with two coffees in your hand
and that sweet smile on your face.
You are my Evergreen.
Undeniably true.

And no matter where our story goes,
I must tell you,
You will always be
Someone I love.
You will always be Evergreen to me.

A NEW SONG

I thought I knew patience
'Til my love grew for you,
'Til my heartbeat was set to a song I loved but never knew,
And I had to learn that each soul has its own way to waltz
as two.

THAT CHRISTMAS FEELING

Rainbow-sugared gumdrops,
Lights on a gingerbread house.
Creamy icing for icicles along the roof.
And her heart is as soft as the red velvet on her skin tonight.
Her spirit finally lifted,
Like a puppy playing in its first snow.

A MIRROR

A mountain lioness came to her,
Nuzzled her close.
While others in the dream were fearful,
She was at peace.
And within the lioness's unique beauty,
Strength and protection,
She saw a mirror into herself,
Her divine, unlike any other femininity and way of being.
And she breathes in,
Her powerful capacity—
To love,
That she is instinctively assured will carry her through
anything at all.

THOUGHTS ON FALLING IN LOVE

Falling in love,
Seems to be,
An ancient forest
With sudden dips,
Curves,
And climbs
Shrouded in an ethereal fog,
That at times clears,
Revealing the brightest and restoring sun.
But you are never completely sure,
When falling in love;
You take a deep breath
And keep taking each step forward,
Trusting in the guidance of your heart
And your angels residing in the heavens above.

HOW I KNOW

I have been around the sun a few times to know what is true.
He does not always speak his love,
But I feel
His connection to me
In the way he is around me,
Always within his kiss
And the way his body relaxes with mine;
In little time, we become under the influence of each other's
soul.
Within his attentiveness to me when we are apart,
We never part.
And that is so very sweet and real to me.
It is how I know,
Beyond surface-level checklists,
And silent hours' insecurities,
Together we are right.

ONE GREAT STORY

He has grown into her,
and she has grown into him;
like roots
close together
intertwine,
neither desiring to look at life
without
a picture of the other.

LOVE IS A DANCE

Love is a dance
of close embrace
to pulling apart for a little room to appreciate
the entirety of her,
the entirety of him.

Love is a dance
of mesmerizing twirls
to contemplative holds with the slightest sway.

Love is a dance,
and if done right,
will synchronize two for the kind of song that is timeless;
for the kind of story,
the kind of love
that lasts on into eternity.

ON A JANUARY MORNING BEFORE SUNRISE

A few lights on homes linger though we are well into the
new year.
We are holding on and letting go
Knowing there will come a time,
Any day now,
When the old will truly be marked as the past;
And thoughts will wander to where we will be
After cherry blossoms and green, and twinkle lights return.
Our hearts will once again be filled with stirred imaginings
we cannot truly fathom
Until reality's tale is fully weaved.

ACKNOWLEDGMENTS

I want to as always thank my family who are without a doubt "Evergreen." I feel the freedom and love to create because of all of you- Mom, Dad, Robbie, Alistair, and all my angels in Heaven. Thank you to my Godfather Clifford Fischer who has been so supportive and encouraging of my poetry, and thank you to Jonathan who has added so much to my life and who I feel blessed to have in my life and story. Thank you also to Harbor Lane Books for believing in my work. And, thank you to God for always guiding me and reminding me through feather-like nudges what I should do and where I should go next. Through my faith, I know that I do not walk alone; You are always beside me.

Christie Leigh Babirad is an award-winning author of fiction and poetry.

The primary hope she has for her readers is that her words and stories comfort and inspire. All her books are available via Amazon, B&N, and through other major retailers.

You can follow her art on social media at the following sites to find out more about her latest projects.

facebook.com/authorchristieleighbabirad
x.com/CLBauthor
instagram.com/christieleighbabiradauthor
youtube.com/@christieleighbabirad1707
goodreads.com/cbabiradauthor

ON THE ROAD OF
Love
POEMS
CHRISTIE LEIGH BABIRAD